W9-BNO-184

3|06

AWESOME VALUES IN FAMOUS LIVES

Oprah Winfrey

Reaching Out to Others

Barbara Kramer

Enslow Elementary
an imprint of
Enslow Publishers, Inc.

40 Industrial Road   PO Box 38
Box 398   Aldershot
Berkeley Heights, NJ 07922 Hants GU12 6BP
USA   UK

http://www.enslow.com

Enslow Elementary, an imprint of Enslow Publishers, Inc.

Enslow Elementary® is a registered trademark of Enslow Publishers, Inc.

Library of Congress Cataloging-in-Publication Data

Kramer, Barbara.
  Oprah Winfrey : reaching out to others / Barbara Kramer.
    p. cm. — (Awesome values in famous lives)
  Includes bibliographical references and index.
  ISBN 0-7660-2378-8 (hardcover)
  1. Winfrey, Oprah—Juvenile literature. 2. Television personalities—United States—Biography—Juvenile literature. 3. Actors—United States—Biography—Juvenile literature. I. Title. II. Series.

PN1992.4.W56K73 2005
794.1502'8'092—dc22

                                                                2004019264

Printed in the United States of America

10 9 8 7 6 5 4 3 2 1

To Our Readers: We have done our best to make sure all Internet Addresses in this book were active and appropriate when we went to press. However, the author and the publisher have no control over and assume no liability for the material available on those Internet sites or on other Web sites they may link to. Any comments or suggestions can be sent by e-mail to comments@enslow.com or to the address on the back cover.

Every effort has been made to locate all copyright holders of material used in this book. If any errors or omissions have occurred, corrections will be made in future editions of this book.

Illustration Credits: © 2005 JupiterImages Corporation, p. 6 (farm); © Corel Corporation, p. 9; AP/Wide World, pp. 2, 4–5, 20, 22, 23, 27, 28, 37, 38, 39, 41, 43; Enslow Publishers, Inc., p. 36; Everett Collection, pp. 21, 29, 31; Globe Photos, Inc., pp. 34–35; Hemera Technologies Inc., pp. 13, 33; Kosciusko Tourist Promotion Council, p. 7; Metropolitan Government Archives of Nashville and Davidson County, pp. 10, 14, 15, 16, 17; NewsChannel 5 Network/Nashville, TN, p. 18; Personal Collection of Oprah Winfrey, p. 6 (childhood photo); Photog/IPOL/Globe Photos, Inc., p. 40; Sara McIntosh Wooten, p. 11; Tim Anderson/Alpha/Globe Photos, p. 32.

Cover Illustration: AP/Wide World.

Contents

CHAPTER 1

A "Gifted" Child

Inside Harpo Studios in Chicago, Illinois, the cameras are ready. The air crackles with excitement. Here comes Oprah Winfrey! The audience for *The Oprah Winfrey Show* cheers and claps wildly. Oprah is one of the richest, most powerful women in America. Thanks to her television

Oprah's job was to feed the pigs and
chickens on her grandmother's farm.

show, she has millions of fans. Yet many people do not
think of her only as a superstar. To them, Oprah seems
like a friend, because she talks to them about her life.

Oprah Gail Winfrey was born on January 29, 1954,
on her grandparents' farm in Kosciusko, Mississippi.
Oprah was only four when her mother, Vernita Lee,
went to Milwaukee, Wisconsin, to find a job. Her father,
Vernon Winfrey, was in the army. Oprah stayed on the
farm with her grandmother.

Oprah's grandmother had strict rules. In those days, children who did not obey often got a beating. "She could whip me for days and never get tired," Oprah said.[1] Still, she knew that her grandmother loved her. Oprah liked sitting on the porch while her grandmother oiled and braided her hair. She told Oprah stories from the Bible and taught her to kneel and say her prayers each night.

When Oprah was three, she discovered that she had a special talent. Oprah loved to stand up and

Oprah went to this church every Sunday with her grandmother.

recite Bible verses in church. The ladies would turn to her grandmother and say, "Hattie Mae, this child is gifted."[2]

In kindergarten, Oprah was bored. She had been reading since she was three years old. Yet her classmates were just learning the alphabet. Oprah wrote a note to her teacher: "Dear Miss Newe. I do not think I belong here."[3] The teacher agreed, and Oprah was moved up to first grade.

At six, Oprah went to Milwaukee to live with her mother, who had a new baby, Patricia. Oprah's mother worked long hours as a maid, but she did not earn much money. The family lived in one crowded room, and life was hard. When Oprah was eight, her mother sent her to stay with

From Orpah to Oprah

How did Oprah get her name? It happened by mistake. When she was born, she was named Orpah, after a woman in the Bible. But somebody spelled the baby's name wrong, mixing up the *r* and the *p*. So *Orpah* became *Oprah*.

The city of Milwaukee was very different
from Grandma Hattie Mae's farm.

Vernon Winfrey, Oprah's dad.

her father. Vernon Winfrey now lived in a house in Nashville, Tennessee, and had a wife named Zelma.

As a third grader in Nashville, Oprah was already trying to help other people. At church, she heard about starving children in the country of Costa Rica. Oprah wanted to help those children. "I used to collect money on the playground every single day of the year," she later said.[4]

At the end of the school year, Oprah went back to live with her mother and Patricia and a new baby, named Jeffrey. That summer, something terrible happened. Oprah was abused by her teenaged cousin. Oprah was only nine years old. She did not understand why he hurt her, but she knew it was wrong.[5] Oprah's cousin said they would both get in trouble if anyone found out. Over the next few years, Oprah was also abused by an uncle and a family friend. She was afraid to tell anyone. This big secret made her feel sad and all alone.[6]

Oprah was unhappy, and she started getting into trouble. She told lies and stole money from her mother's purse. One day she ran away from home and was gone for a whole week. By the time Oprah was fourteen years old, her mother could not control her anymore. Vernita did not know what to do. She called Oprah's father and asked him to come get Oprah.

Vernon's barbershop in Nashville.

WINFREYS BARBER SHOP

Winfrey's BEAUTY SHOP

CHAPTER 2

A New Start

Oprah's father would not put up with her wild ways. He made her throw out her short, tight skirts and wash off her thick makeup. Oprah had to be home early at night. Television was limited to one hour a day. The rest of the time was for schoolwork— and he expected Oprah to get A's on her report card. Oprah knew that her father was right. "My father saved me," she said.[1]

Oprah acted in school plays at East Nashville High School. She also performed in churches all around Nashville. She liked to recite the words of famous African-American women from her favorite books. When she was fifteen, she was invited to California to speak to church groups there. "Other people were known for singing; I was known for talking," she said.[3]

In her last year of high school, Oprah got a part-time job at a radio station in Nashville. She worked after school and on weekends, reading the news on the radio. When the Nashville fire department held a beauty contest to choose Miss Fire Prevention, Oprah

Hitch Up a Mosquito

Oprah's father expected her to follow his rules. "Listen, girl, if I tell you a mosquito can pull a wagon, don't ask me no questions. Just hitch him up!" he told Oprah.[2]

Who will win the Miss Fire Prevention contest?

decided to enter. The girls had to wear fancy dresses and answer questions from the judges. One question was, "What would you do if you had a million dollars?"

The first girl said that she would use the money to help the poor. The second girl said she would help her family. Then it was Oprah's turn. "I'd be a spending *fool*!" she said.[4] The judges liked Oprah for being so honest and funny. She won the contest and was the first African American to be named Nashville's Miss Fire Prevention.

Oprah graduated from high school in 1971. That fall she started classes at Tennessee State University. She studied speech and acting and dreamed of

It's Oprah! Miss Fire Prevention waves to the crowd.

At East Nashville High School, Oprah, center front, was vice president of the student council.

becoming an actress. In 1972, Oprah won two more beauty contests. She was named Miss Black Nashville, then Miss Black Tennessee. She also still worked at the radio station.

In 1973, when Oprah was nineteen, she was hired by WTVF, the CBS television station in Nashville. She became the station's first African-American news co-anchor, one of the two main reporters on the television news show. Oprah liked being in front of the camera. She had an excellent voice. She kept on working part-time while she was in college.

Oprah's high school yearbook photo.

After a few years, Oprah was offered a job at WJZ, the ABC-TV station in Baltimore, Maryland. The station asked

Oprah was the youngest person—and the first African-American woman—to co-host the news on WTVF-TV.

her to be a reporter and co-anchor of the evening news. Oprah was in her last year of college. She hated to quit school when she was so close to finishing. But she liked the idea of getting out on her own. Oprah was twenty-two years old and still living at home under her father's strict rules.

The job was also a big career move. Baltimore was a larger city, and the station had more viewers. It was a great opportunity, and Oprah wanted to give it a try. But was it the right job for her?

CHAPTER 3

People Are Talking

Part of Oprah's new job was gathering news. She went into the streets of Baltimore to do on-the-scene reports. With the cameras rolling, she had to question people who had been in accidents or who had been robbed. Oprah could not do it. "I just broke down and cried," she said.[1] That was not how a reporter should act.

Oprah made mistakes as a news anchor.

Oprah also made some mistakes reading the news. On one show, she said the word *Canada* wrong. Instead of *CAN-a-duh*, she said *Ca-NAHD-uh*. The station managers told Oprah to do a better job. They said she must change her looks, too. They sent Oprah to New York City for a makeover. At the hair salon, the stylist used a product that burned her scalp and made her hair fall out. "I had two little spriggles, like a bald man," Oprah said.[2]

Oprah was taken off the evening news show. For a while, she gave some short news reports on the daytime news. Then the station started a new talk show, *People Are Talking*. Oprah became one of the hosts. The show quickly became a success. At last, Oprah had found the perfect job for her talents.

Talking with guests on the show felt so easy. "It's like breathing to me," she said.[3]

Oprah co-hosted *People Are Talking* for six years. By then she was ready for a change. In January 1984, Oprah moved to Chicago to become the host of a talk show called *A.M. Chicago*.

Oprah loved her new job as a talk-show host.

Oprah also got a chance to try acting. One of her favorite books, *The Color Purple* by Alice Walker, was being made into a movie. Oprah flew to Hollywood to try out for a part. She was thrilled when director Steven Spielberg chose her to play a character named Sophia. In the summer of 1985, Oprah took three months off from *A.M. Chicago* to work on the movie.

Oprah takes a minute to relax in her office.

As a child, Oprah had dreamed of acting. She got her wish in *The Color Purple*.

The television station showed reruns and hired guest hosts to fill in while she was gone. When *The Color Purple* opened in movie theaters, newspaper and magazine writers praised Oprah's wonderful acting.

In September 1985, *A.M. Chicago* was given a new name: *The Oprah Winfrey Show*. An even bigger change was about to take place: *A.M. Chicago* was on TV only in the Chicago area. Starting in September 1986, *The Oprah Winfrey Show* would be broadcast in more than one hundred cities across the United States. Soon people all over the country would be able to see Oprah on television.

Talk-show host, movie actress, what would Oprah do next?

For Oprah, it was an exciting time, and it made her think about the future. "I wonder how it will change my life?" she wrote in her journal that day.[4]

CHAPTER 4

Kicking Off Her Shoes

In 1986, Oprah was given a small role in another movie, *Native Son*. It was based on a famous book by Richard Wright. Acting in movies was fun, but Oprah had even bigger ideas. She wanted to be in charge of making movies from start to finish. To do that, she founded her own company, called Harpo, Inc. The name *Harpo* is "Oprah" spelled backward. Then she spent about $20 million to buy a building in Chicago and fix it up for the company offices. It would take a couple of years until Harpo Studios was ready.

Why is Oprah's talk show such a huge hit with millions of fans? Oprah understands her viewers. She knows what they wonder about, and she asks the right questions. Oprah laughs with her guests, and sometimes cries with them. She listens with her heart, and she shares her own experiences.

Oprah likes to relax and enjoy herself, too. "If I can't be myself and take my shoes off when my feet hurt, then I'm not going to do very well," she said.[1]

"Mr. Right"

Over the years, people often asked Oprah why she did not have a special man in her life. She said that she had not met the right person. "Mr. Right's coming, but he's in Africa and he's walking," she once said.[2] (She was joking that it would take a *long* time for him to arrive.) Oprah found love in 1986 when she met businessman Stedman Graham Jr. They have enjoyed a happy relationship for many years.

In 1987, Oprah won the first of many Emmy Awards as best talk-show host. Winning an Emmy is the highest honor for a television show.

Oprah was successful beyond her wildest dreams, yet she had never finished her last class of college. That upset her. She talked to the people in charge at Tennessee State University. They said she could

Oprah and Stedman.

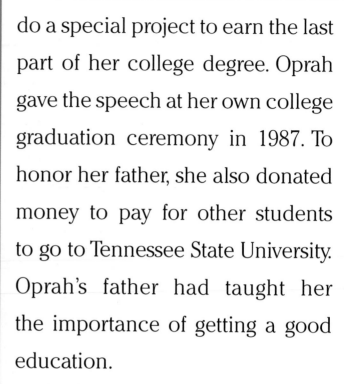

To Oprah, education is very important. "The ability to read saved my life," she said.[3] Here, Oprah gives a speech to other students finishing college.

do a special project to earn the last part of her college degree. Oprah gave the speech at her own college graduation ceremony in 1987. To honor her father, she also donated money to pay for other students to go to Tennessee State University. Oprah's father had taught her the importance of getting a good education.

In 1988, Oprah's company bought *The Oprah Winfrey Show*. This gave Oprah complete control of her television program. Harpo Studios covers a whole block, with offices and a stage where *The Oprah Winfrey Show* is filmed. The building also

Oprah does not hide her feelings. She laughs and cries with the guests on her television show.

has a fitness center, a cafeteria, and plenty of room for making movies. Since 1988, Harpo has made a series called *The Women of Brewster Place* and television movies based on some of Oprah's favorite books. Other projects are in the works as well. Harpo Films, in Los Angeles, California, is another of Oprah's companies for making movies.

By 1998, Oprah and her show had won thirty-nine Emmy Awards, including a Lifetime Achievement Award for all that Oprah had done.

Owning her own show and movie studios has made Oprah very rich. She enjoys using some of her money to surprise her friends and the people who work for her. One time, Oprah handed out rolls of

Oprah and the cast of *The Women of Brewster Place*.

Oprah gets lots of exercise and eats healthy foods.
She likes to go jogging with fitness expert Bob Greene.

toilet paper to seven people on her staff. It seemed like a strange gift at first. But inside each of the rolls, she had stuffed $10,000 in cash. "It feels good to be able to do things like that," she said.[4] Another time, Oprah took four staff members on a grand shopping spree in New York City. She hired a driver to take them from store to store. Oprah paid for everything.

Even more important, Oprah uses her money to help people in need. She is very generous in donating to many charities. She has given millions of dollars to libraries, colleges, and programs to help poor or sick children.

Stopping Child Abuse

In 1990, on *The Oprah Winfrey Show*, Oprah told the world about the abuse she suffered as a child. Abuse must *never* be kept secret, she said. Children must always tell a teacher or other grown-up who will help them.

Oprah talked to some lawmakers in Washington, D.C. A new law, called the National Child Protection Act, was passed in 1993.

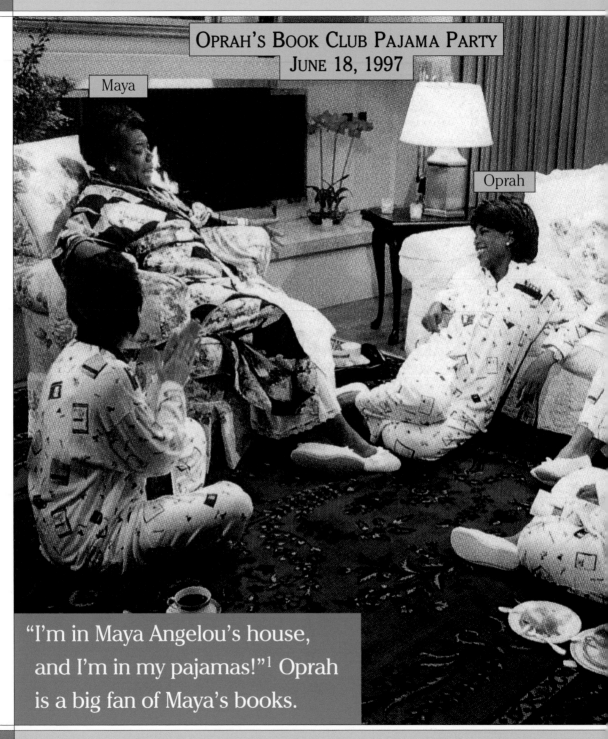

Maya

Oprah

"I'm in Maya Angelou's house, and I'm in my pajamas!"[1] Oprah is a big fan of Maya's books.

CHAPTER 5

Helping Others

Oprah loves to read, and she believes it is important for everyone. In 1996, she started Oprah's Book Club to make reading part of her show. About once a month, Oprah picked a book that she wanted to share with her viewers. Then she invited the author of the book to be a guest on her show. Oprah's fans were excited about reading books

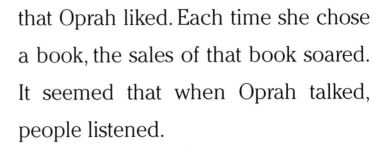

that Oprah liked. Each time she chose a book, the sales of that book soared. It seemed that when Oprah talked, people listened.

Could Oprah's words get her into trouble, too? One day in 1996, *The Oprah Winfrey Show* was about foods that could make people sick. Oprah listened to an expert talk about mad cow disease. Then she blurted out, "It has just stopped me cold from eating another burger."[2] Some cattle ranchers in Texas were angry. They said many people did not buy beef after the show, and they blamed Oprah.

Oprah believes in free speech— the right to say what is on her mind. In court, her lawyers argued against the cattle ranchers. The trial lasted a whole month, but Oprah came out a winner. Outside the courtroom she pumped her fists in the air and shouted, "Free speech not only lives, it rocks."[3]

"Not guilty!" said the jury.

Oprah cares very deeply about other people. In 1998 she started Oprah's Angel Network to encourage everyone to help make a better world. One part of Oprah's Angel Network was the World's Largest Piggy Bank. Oprah asked people to send in nickels and dimes—any change they could spare. In just one year, all the coins added up to more than $1 million. The money was used to send needy students to college.

In December 2002, Oprah had an idea that seemed too big even for her. She wanted to give

"It was the best day of my life," said Oprah,
"just to see the joy on these kids' faces."[4]

Oprah has helped so many children in South Africa.

50,000 African children a Christmas they would always remember. She and a team of volunteers traveled to South Africa. They spent three weeks visiting schools and orphanages. They also hosted parties for thousands of children in a huge white tent.

Some of the children walked many miles to come to the parties. They had no shoes to protect their feet. Oprah greeted them with a smile and a hug. They ate, danced, and played games. Every child received gifts

O, The Oprah Magazine

In the spring of 2000, Oprah started her own magazine, called *O, The Oprah Magazine.* "O is what a lot of my friends call me," she said.[5] It gives readers many ideas about how they can live better lives. Oprah is also part owner of the Oxygen Network on cable television.

of clothes, books, toys, and school supplies. They all got brand-new tennis shoes.

Oprah did not stop there. She also donated millions of dollars to build a school where girls can live and study near the city of Johannesburg, South Africa.

Oprah is always finding new ways to help others. She does that best through her own television talk show. That is because she has so many fans. About 30 million people across the United States watch the show every week. It is also seen in more than one hundred countries all around the world.

In 2004, Oprah announced that *The Oprah Winfrey Show* would be on television at least until the year 2011.

Oprah has won many awards for her talk show and for all her good deeds.

Oprah is always finding new ways to help others.

To Oprah, bringing her show into so many homes each day is a gift. "I'm in a position to change people's lives," she said.[6]

It is exciting work that Oprah wants to keep on doing for a long time.

Timeline

1954   Born on January 29 in Kosciusko, Mississippi.

1971   Begins work as a newscaster at a radio station in Nashville, Tennessee.

1973   Gets a job as a television news anchor in Nashville.

1976   Begins work as a news anchor for the six o'clock news at WJZ-TV in Baltimore, Maryland.

1978   Begins co-hosting a new talk show, *People Are Talking*.

1984   Moves to Chicago, Illinois, to host a talk show called *A.M. Chicago* at WLS-TV.

1986   Forms her own company: Harpo, Inc.

1988   Becomes the owner of *The Oprah Winfrey Show*.

1998   Starts Oprah's Angel Network to encourage people to help one another.

2000   Starts her magazine, *O, The Oprah Magazine*.

2004   Announces that *The Oprah Winfrey Show* will continue through 2011.

"I feel blessed," says Oprah Winfrey.[7]

Words to Know

abuse—To hurt or harm someone.

career—The kind of work a person does to earn a living.

charity—A group of people or a fund of money that helps needy people.

donate—To give as a gift.

mad cow disease—A very rare but deadly sickness that destroys the brain.

makeover—Changing people's hair and clothes to give them a new look.

orphanage—A home that cares for children who have no parents.

recite—To repeat or perform something learned by memory, usually for an audience.

volunteer—A person who chooses to do work or a service without being paid for it.

Chapter Notes

CHAPTER 1.
A "Gifted" Child

1. Alan Richman, "Oprah," *People*, January 12, 1987, p. 50.

2. Linda Peterson, "Oprah: She Came, She Talked, She Conquered," *Biography Magazine*, March 1999, p. 42.

3. Oprah Winfrey, "What I Know for Sure," *O, The Oprah Magazine*, September 2000, p. 320.

4. Robert Waldron, *Oprah!* (New York: St. Martin's Press, 1987), p. 32.

5. Barbara Walters, "Oprah Winfrey," *Ladies' Home Journal Special: Barbara Walters' Best Interviews*, July 17, 1994, p. 15.

6. Lynette Clemetson, "'It Is Constant Work': Oprah on Staying Centered, Ambition, Letting Go—and Pajamas," *Newsweek*, January 8, 2001, p. 45.

CHAPTER 2.
A New Start

1. Robert Waldron, *Oprah!* (New York: St. Martin's Press, 1987), p. 43.

2. Norman King, "Oprah," *Good Housekeeping*, August 1987, p. 178.

3. The Hall of Business, Interview, February 21, 1991, <http://www.achievement.org> (January 15, 2004).

4. King, p. 178.

CHAPTER 3.
People Are Talking

1. Judy Markey, "Brassy Sassy Oprah Winfrey," *Cosmopolitan*, September 1986, p. 99.

2. "Oprah Winfrey," *People*, May 12, 1997, p. 115.

Chapter Notes

3. Chris Andersen, "Meet Oprah Winfrey," *Good Housekeeping*, August 1986, p. 37.

4. Audrey Edwards, "The O Factor," *Essence*, October 2003, p. 178.

CHAPTER 4.
Kicking Off Her Shoes

1. Pamela Noel, "Lights! Camera! Oprah!" *Ebony*, April 1985, p. 105.

2. Elizabeth Sporkin, "Her Man Stedman," *People*, November 23, 1992, p. 134.

3. "Academy of Achievement Oprah Winfrey Interview," <http://www.achievement.org> (January 26, 2005).

4. Charles Whitaker, "Oprah Winfrey: The Most Talked-About TV Talk Show Host," *Ebony*, March 1987, p. 44.

CHAPTER 5.
Helping Others

1. *The Oprah Winfrey Show*, ABC-TV, June 18, 1997, transcript, p. 1.

2. "Texas Cattlemen Lose Suit Against Oprah," CNN online, February 26, 1998, <http://www.cnn.com/US/9802/26/oprah.trial> (July 7, 2005).

3. Janet Lowe, *Oprah Winfrey Speaks: Insight from the World's Most Influential Voice*, New York: John Wiley & Sons, Inc., 1998, p. 139.

4. "Oprah Winfrey Hosts HOPE *worldwide* Party in Soweto," © 2001 HOPE *worldwide*, <http://hopeww.org/home/2002/12/oprah.htm> (October 25, 2004).

5. "Oprah Winfrey Magazine Named: 'O, The Oprah Magazine,'" *The Write News*, January 12, 2000, <http://www.writenews.com/2000/011200_o_oprah.htm> (June 17, 2005).

6. The Hall of Business, Interview, February 21, 1991, <http://www.achievement.org> (January 15, 2004).

7. (p. 43) "Academy of Achievement Oprah Winfrey Interview," <http://www.achievement.org> (January 26, 2005).

Learn More

Books

Blashfield, Jean F. *Oprah Winfrey*. Milwaukee, Wisc.:
World Almanac Library, 2003.

Guilfoyle, Peg. *Oprah Winfrey*. Mankato, Minn.:
Creative Education, 2000.

Ward, Kristin. *Learning About Assertiveness from the Life of
Oprah Winfrey*. New York: Powerkids Press, 2001.

Wheeler, Jill C. *Oprah Winfrey*. Minneapolis, Minn.:
Abdo & Daughters, 2002.

Internet Addresses

Type Oprah's name into the search box at this web site
to read more about Oprah and to see photos of her life
and career.
<http://www.achievement.org>

Oprah's official web site has news about Oprah; *The Oprah
Winfrey Show; O, The Oprah Magazine;* and Oprah's Angel
Network. Video clips show Oprah chatting with her studio
audience on a show called *Oprah After the Show*.
<http://www.oprah.com>

Index

Pages with photographs are in **boldface** type.